30 DAYS OF EMPATHETIC LEADERSHIP!

(The Art Of Meaningful Connections)

BY TODD M. SIMMONS

30 DAYS OF EMPATHETIC LEADERSHIP!

(The Art Of Meaningful Connections)

BY TODD M. SIMMONS

ISBN: 979-88347-58389

30 DAYS OF EMPATHETIC LEADERSHIP!

(The Art Of Meaningful Connections)

BY TODD M. SIMMONS

FOR YOU...

FOREWORD

"Empathy is the capacity to understand or feel what another person is experiencing from within their frame of reference, that is, the capacity to place oneself in another's position."

The importance of empathy was first introduced by Dr. Brené Brown. She emphasized that empathy can be used to create meaning and belonging in our lives. It helps us recognize the individuality of others and understand their perspectives on any given experience. And this understanding allows us to connect with them, collaborate with them more effectively, and ultimately lead happier lives for ourselves. Dr. Brown specifically asserted that an "empathy deficit" is at the root of many of society's ills today - from bullying to racism to sexism, these issues stem from a lack of understanding and appreciation for difference (Brown).

Empathy is the ability to understand and share the feelings of another. It is an important skill for people who work in customer service and management. It is also a key component of good leadership.

The importance of empathy has been highlighted

in recent years by psychologists, neuroscientists, and sociologists. They say that empathy can be developed by practicing it over time, but it can't be developed with just one experience or interaction.

Simply put, can you see me?

DAY 1

EMPATHETIC LEADERS ARE SELF-AWARE

Self-aware leaders are leaders who know and understand their own strengths and weaknesses. They also understand the strengths and weaknesses of their team members.

"Empathy is a special way of coming to know another and ourselves."

CARL R. ROGERS

As self-aware leaders, they focus on the people they lead and on what it takes to be a good leader. They can use these skills to motivate their team members to perform better. These leaders also build relationships with their team members through open dialogue about goals, successes, failures, challenges, and frustrations. We have a responsibility to recognize the self-awareness of leaders and to understand how it can be applied to create more effective leadership.

Self-awareness is about being aware of ourselves and our environment. It's the difference between me and we.

The more we're able to see our strengths, weaknesses, and blind spots, the more we're able to approach life with intentionality.

There are several steps that leaders can take to increase their self-awareness:

1. Identify their values.
2. Understand what's getting in their way.
3. Make time for reflection and introspection.
4. Allow themselves some time away from work (to recharge).

Self-Assessment Questions:

1. What are my strengths?
2. Do I have any weakness?
3. What kind of person am I?
4. How well do I know the strength and weakness of my employees or followers?
5. How do I approach problems?

Rate Yourself:

1	2	3	4	5	6

Needs improvement   Crushing it

DAY 2

EMPATHETIC LEADERS LISTEN

Listening is the act of hearing someone with intent to understand. Empathetic leaders listen. They have the ability to not only hear what is being said, but also what is left unsaid. This skill takes a lot of work and practice. It requires a lot of patience and a desire for understanding other people's perspectives, ideas, and feelings.

"Empathy is seeing with the eyes of another, listening with the ears of another and feeling with the eyes of another."

ALFRED ADLER

Listening is a critical skill for leaders because it allows them to be in touch with their team members' perspectives, ideas, and feelings from their point of view. When leaders listen well, they are more likely to take appropriate actions that benefit the team as a whole rather than just themselves or their own department or division.

Empathetic leaders listen to their employees and take

DAY 3

EMPATHETIC LEADERS BUILD TRUST

A good leader builds a trusting relationship with the people they lead. Trust is a positive form of a psychological contract between leaders and their followers. Leaders who have developed a reputation for being trustworthy have the ability to influence their followers not only through information and rewards, but also through the promise of psychological safety.

"Trust is the essence of Leadership."

COLIN POWELL

As such, trust can be seen as "a kind of social glue that cements relationships and facilitates cooperation among diverse individuals." Leadership is an act of trust. A good leader builds trust by following through on promises, giving honest feedback, and helping employees grow in their careers.

Empathetic leaders can't build trust without honesty, transparency, integrity, respect, and reliability. Leaders should be willing to be vulnerable when it comes to being trustworthy because being vulnerable is the only way people will show you vulnerability in return. Leaders have to be willing to give away their power so that we can get it back in return. We all have the ability to earn trust.

Good leaders build trust by:

1. Holding themselves accountable.
2. Sharing credit with team members.
3. Being honest and transparent.

Self-Assessment Questions:

1. How honest am I with my team members?
2. Do I share credits with them?
3. How transparent am I?
4. Do my employees trust me?
5. How can I earn their trust?

Rate Yourself:

1	2	3	4	5	6

Needs improvement   Crushing it

DAY 4

EMPATHETIC LEADERS ARE
APPROACHABLE

Good leaders possess a certain quality - being approachable. This makes it easier for their followers to communicate with them and also understand their needs. The good leaders will not only listen to the opinions of the followers, but also try to understand their problems and offer a solution.

"A leader is one who knows the way, goes the way and shows the way."

JOHN MAXWELL

Being approachable is an important charactcristic of good leadership. It makes it easier for people to communicate with you and also understand your needs. Good leaders will not only listen to the opinions of their followers, but they'll also try to understand their problems and offer a solution, too.

Good leaders create a sense of trust and respect

among the members of their organization. They want people to feel welcomed and comfortable in their workplace so that they can get the most out of them both personally and professionally.

In order for leaders to create this atmosphere among the staff, they need to demonstrate all of these qualities: empathy, assertiveness, consistency, respectfulness, availability, and warmth. They need to make their presence known and reach out. They need to keep in mind what will benefit the team and do a lot of listening. A good leader is not afraid of feedback and criticism from their employees because that only helps them grow as a person, learn from mistakes, and become better at their job. A good communicator will always tell you what's on their mind so there is no room for assumptions.

Self-Assessment Questions:

1. How often do my employees approach me to solve a problem?
2. Am I always available when they need me?
3. Do I solve their problems when I can?
4. Are they comfortable approaching me?
5. How easy is it for them to approach me?

Rate Yourself:

1	2	3	4	5	6

Needs improvement   Crushing it

DAY 5

EMPATHETIC LEADERS ARE MOTIVATORS

A good leader is a motivator. A good leader knows that an organization's culture starts with the beliefs, values, and assumptions of the leadership. A motivating leader can create a positive environment for their employees. They know how to inspire people to work hard and be creative.

"If your actions inspire others to dream more, learn more, do more and become more, then you're a leader."

JOHN QUINCY ADAMS

Motivating leaders are also inspiring leaders. They know how to use emotional intelligence to communicate with people in a way that they would feel respected and appreciated. Leaders who are not afraid of risks are highly motivated to take on new challenges.

Research has shown that there are three qualities of a good leader. They are:

1. Inspiring a shared vision.
2. Enabling others to act.
3. Motivating action and performance.

Self-Assessment Questions:

1. Am I a motivator?
2. How often do I encourage my team?
3. Do I inspire them to work hard?
4. Do I inspire them to become more?
5. How can I inspire my team?

Rate Yourself:

1	2	3	4	5	6

Needs improvement   Crushing it

DAY 6

EMPATHETIC LEADERS ARE FLEXIBLE

Leadership is not about one specific style or philosophy. Flexible leadership skills are an asset to any leader. A good leader must be able to be flexible in their management style. They can't rely solely on their own way of tackling problems, but instead they need to try different styles and see what works best for each situation. For example, if a boss is facing resistance from an employee, they could try communicating with them respectfully and show understanding for the employee's issues before moving onto more aggressive measures like yelling at them or trying to force them into submission.

"Be clear about your goal but be flexible about the process of achieving it."

BRIAN TRACY

Flexible leaders are known for their ability to be flexible and improvise. They can do this because they have a vision that is bigger than the obstacles they face. This flexibility is what separates good leaders from great leaders. Flexible leaders can navigate through difficult situations and be flexible in their approach.

This can be done with the help of two approaches:

The first is to monitor your thoughts, reactions, and emotions to make sure they are congruent with what you want (the golden rule). The second is monitoring your thoughts for ideas on how to deal with the situation.

Self-Assessment Questions:

1. What is my style of leadership?
2. Do I rely only on my way of solving problems?
3. How well can I navigate difficult situations?
4. Do I monitor my thoughts?
5. How can I be a flexible leader?

Rate Yourself:

1	2	3	4	5	6

Needs improvement   Crushing it

DAY 7

EMPATHETIC LEADERS ARE COURAGEOUS

Courageous leaders are not afraid to take risks. They are not afraid to change the status quo and they are not afraid to do what's right, no matter the obstacles that they may face. Leaders who demonstrate these qualities will not only be able to successfully lead the team, but also inspire others.

"I think we all have empathy. We may not have enough courage to display it."

MAYA ANGELO

Courageous leaders can take risks and do not shy away from difficult decisions. They are confident and even when they don't know the answer, they will say so. A leader with courage will have a positive impact on their employees, their company, and the world. They will be able to motivate people who don't want to lead or those who just can't do it anymore.

Anyone who wants to lead should be courageous. "It takes courage to make decisions in the face of uncertainty, to act in the face of obstacles, and to persevere in the face of adversity.

Empathetic leaders are uniquely positioned for this type of courage since they must be willing to forge their own path rather than following others. Good leaders are courageous because without courage, there can't be effective leadership.

Self-Assessment Questions:

1. Am I a courageous leader?
2. How often do I take risks?
3. Do I make decisions in the face of uncertainty?
4. What positive impact do I have in my team?
5. How can I successfully lead my team?

Rate Yourself:

1	2	3	4	5	6

Needs improvement   Crushing it

DAY 8

EMPATHETIC LEADERSHIP COMES
WITH RISKS

Leaders are expected to lead others. They are responsible for the success of their followers. Empathetic leaders put themselves in their follower's shoes and try to understand their emotions, needs, motivations, and expectations. But is it risky?

"The men who have done big things are those who were not afraid to attempt big things, who were not afraid to risk failure in order to gain success."

B.C. FORBES

Empathy in leadership can be very risky in many ways. There are many risks that come with being an empathetic leader. Leaders must ensure they are exercising a healthy balance, creating a culture of accountability and compassion.

Self-Assessment Questions:

1. Am I afraid to take risks?
2. Can I handle tough situations?
3. Do I have the qualities of an empathetic leader?
4. Have I ever shown empathy?
5. What greatest risk have I taken as a leader?

Rate Yourself:

1	2	3	4	5	6

Needs improvement   Crushing it

DAY 9

EMPATHETIC LEADERS COMMUNICATE

In today's fast-paced world, it is important to be able to communicate with others quickly and efficiently. This becomes more difficult when you are not in the same physical space as the person you are communicating with. Leadership skills can be enhanced through a few simple steps that can help you to better connect with your team and customers.

"Empathy is simply listening, holding space, withholding judgment, emotionally connecting, and communicating that incredibly healing message of you're not alone."

BRENÉ BROWN

Be a good listener: Listen carefully to what people have to say and practice active listening skills. This will allow you to understand the needs of your team members or customers, which will contribute to better communication in the future.

Create an open environment: As a leader, it is important for you to create an environment where people feel comfortable sharing their ideas and opinions without fear of judgement or criticism. Create this environment by listening attentively and responding positively.

Self-Assessment Questions:

1. Am I a good listener?
2. How well do I communicate with my employees?
3. Does my team communicate their problems to me?
4. Does I let them share their opinion?
5. Have I ever stopped them from communicating with me?

Rate Yourself:

1	2	3	4	5	6
Needs improvement					Crushing it

DAY 10

EMPATHETIC LEADERS SET THE TONE

Get comfortable with discomfort.

There will be easy days and hard days. Regardless, make them all count and do not rely on the easy days to carry you through the hard days. Every day should bring some discomfort. Tackle the hard issues and do not wait.

Set realistic goals that energize the workforce. How much buy-in do they have to organizational success? Goals are reinforced through setting productive organizational culture and not just through a memo on the breakroom bulletin board.

Become the person others want to help.

Mimic the culture you want to set in the organization. If you are not a living breathing example of the organizational culture to the best of your ability, why would anyone else feel they need to?

Self-Assessment Questions:

1. Do I lead by example?
2. Do I set realistic goals?
3. How often do I achieve my goals when I set them?
4. Am I comfortable with discomfort?
5. How can I lead by example?

Writing prompts:

1. Are you aware of your strengths and weaknesses? Write down your strengths and weaknesses.
2. How often do you listen to your employees? Write down how you can be approachable and three ways you can listen without interrupting.
3. How trustworthy are you? Do your employees trust you? What ways can you build trust with your employees?
4. Have you ever failed to communicate with your team? Why? Write down ways you can build effective communication with your team.

5. Do you set the tone? Do you encourage your employees? Write down five ways to motivate your team.

Self-Assessment Questions:

1. Am I afraid to take risks?
2. Do I set the tone?
3. Have I ever shown empathy?
4. What greatest risk have I taken as a leader?

Rate Yourself:

1	2	3	4	5	6

Needs improvement   Crushing it

DAY 11

EMPATHETIC LEADERS ARE KIND

There is strength in kindness. A good leader is kind to the people they lead. Kind and empathetic leaders treat their followers or employees like humans. They understand that these people are adults and not children. Kind leaders smile, they give sincere feedback, they say thank you when necessary and talk politely. They think before they talk and take action.

"There is no greater intelligence than kindness and empathy."

BRYANT H. MCGILL

Kind leadership gives rise to the elements of authenticity, clarity, and warmth.

A kind empathetic leader is kind with their words. They say things that will not hurt the feelings of the people they lead. Being kind with your words is a trait of an empathetic leader.

Kindness does not mean weakness. A kind empathetic leader is kind with their actions. You can make difficult transparent decisions and take tough action while being kind. You must communicate as much as you can in a clear tone.

Being a kind leader not only encourages growth but facilitates a happier and more productive workforce.

When people strive to make ends meet, the best thing you can do for them is to be kind. Do not forget to be kind to yourself as well.

Self-Assessment Questions:

1. Do I talk politely?
2. Am I kind with my actions?
3. Have I ever said something that hurt my employee?
4. How often do I say kind words?
5. Do I think before I talk?

Rate Yourself:

1	2	3	4	5	6

Needs improvement · Crushing it

DAY 12

EMPATHETIC LEADERS ARE SENSITIVE

Great leaders are sensitive. They understand and know every one of their followers. They know what every one of them is capable of. Empathetic leaders are sensitive to the needs of their employees.

"Stay connected to feel empathy, compassion and understanding for yourself and others."

VANESSA TUCKER

A sensitive leader knows when an employee or follower is in a sad mood. An empathetic, sensitive leader who knows this finds a way to cheer them up. Or tries not to worsen their mood. Being sensitive as a leader helps you maximize effective leadership.

Being sensitive as a leader shows you are caring, observant, considerate, and prudent. As an empathetic leader, you must be sensitive towards the feelings of your employees or followers. You can do this by showing concern towards their desires, moods, interest, plans, and inspiration.

Sensitive leaders know when their employee needs a break from work.

A lot of leaders think that being sensitive makes them a coward, but it doesn't. Instead, it helps to build trust. One great way to improve your sensitivity as a leader is by being observant. Communicating and listening are other ways to improve your sensitivity.

Paying attention to nonverbal cues such as gestures and facial expressions also helps you sense when something is wrong with any of your employees. It also helps you to know when you have said or done something wrong to them.

Self-Assessment Questions:

1. Do I know what each of my employees are capable of?
2. How can I be sensitive to their needs?
3. How observant am I?
4. Do I know when an employee needs help?
5. Have I ever been insensitive towards them?

Rate Yourself:

1	2	3	4	5	6

Needs improvement   Crushing it

DAY 13

EMPATHETIC LEADERS ARE APPRECIATIVE

"Thank you," "I appreciate you."

Empathetic leaders use these words when needed. They do not only use it to appreciate their employees, but also to appreciate their customers. Employees may be doing their job but saying those words mean you recognize their hard work, especially when they do something spectacular. Gratitude builds resilience at the workplace.

"To add value to others, one must first value others."

JOHN MAXWELL

If you appreciate an employee when they carry out a herculean task in an excellent way, other employees will always strive to do whatever they are asked to do perfectly to receive your praise. If a task is well executed, you can show appreciation using a gift. There's this joy a person feels when someone recognizes how well you did something and knows you deserve an outstanding recognition. It shows how much they value you and what you have done for them. It keeps you focused to succeed and builds your self-esteem.

Being appreciative as a leader a leader not only shows empathy, it also shows you watch what employees do and how they get it done. It makes them feel seen and recognized.

A leader who is appreciative builds strong and committed relationships with their employees and customers. Moreover, when people are appreciated, they feel happy and work harder. Give your employees credit when they deserve it.

Self-Assessment Questions:

1. Do I say thank you when I need to?
2. How often do I appreciate my team?
3. Do I recognize their hard work?
4. How do I commend them when they complete their task?
5. Have I ever made them feel less appreciated?

Rate Yourself:

1	2	3	4	5	6

Needs improvement   Crushing it

DAY 14

EMPATHETIC LEADERS ARE
EMOTIONALLY INTELLIGENT

A leader who is emotionally intelligent has the ability to acknowledge, understand, and manage their emotions. They not only understand their emotions, but also that of their employees. They act without emotions. A good leader is intelligent, but a great leader is emotionally intelligent.

"True empathy requires that you step outside of your own emotions to view things entirely from the perspective of the other person."

ANONYMOUS

An emotionally intelligent leader is compassionate but doesn't let their emotions get the better of them. They know how to deal with their emotions properly. They are self-aware of their emotions and know how to manage it.

More so, they are also aware of the emotions of their

employees. They know when their employees are sad and when they are happy. They know how to deal with the emotions of each of their employees. They are aware that everyone is different.

Being emotionally intelligent helps leaders manage their team without causing conflict. They know how to get the most out of their employees despite their different personalities.

It also helps maintain a positive and productive workplace. You make difficult decisions irrespective of your emotions. When a leader lacks emotional intelligence, they find it difficult to work and communicate effectively with their employees.

Self-Assessment Questions:

1. Do I know how to manage my emotions?
2. Have I been emotionally intelligent?
3. How can I be conscious of the emotions of my employees?
4. Do I know when they are unhappy?
5. Do I know how to get the most out of my employees?

Rate Yourself:

1   2   3   4   5   6

Needs improvement   Crushing it

DAY 15

EMPATHETIC LEADERS ARE SELFLESS

A leader is someone who cares for his staff as much as he cares for himself. A selfish leader is an awful leader. Being selfish as a leader means you do not care about the needs and demands of your employees. It, however, means that you care only for yourself. Therefore, when making decisions, you think of yourself first and do not consider your employees.

"Empathy is the ability to step outside of your bubble and into the bubble of other people."

C. JOYBELL

When a leader is selfless, they put their team first. He puts the success of their organization and the people he leads first. They don't ask "what is in it for me?" before making a decision or agreeing to a deal. Instead, they ask "what's in it for us?" How can this deal elevate our organization and my team?"
A selfless leader does not take credit for a task their team accomplished but gives credit to everyone on

the team who helped them carry out the task. He doesn't focus on achieving a goal to the detriment of his employees.

Everyone wants to work with a selfless leader. They are honest and know how to pull their organization from a tight situation. You must be courageous and unafraid.

Self-Assessment Questions:

1. Do I put my team before myself?
2. Have I ever taken credit for something an employee did?
3. How can I care about the needs of my team?
4. Do I pay myself before I pay my team?
5. Do I think about how the success of the organization affects them?

Rate Yourself:

1	2	3	4	5	6

Needs improvement   Crushing it

DAY 16

EMPATHETIC LEADERSHIP
BUILDS RELATIONSHIPS

What kind of relationship do you have with your team as a leader? A great leader has a good relationship with every one of their employees. They are curious about the lives of those who work for them. They want to know if their families are fine and if they have any challenges. They are aware of their dreams and aspirations and want to help them achieve them.

"Leadership is about empathy; it is about having the ability to relate to and connect with people for the purpose of inspiring their life."

OPRAH WINFREY

Having a good relationship with your employees helps them work better. It helps them work efficiently and achieve shared goals. Besides, it helps them give honest feedback since they are relaxed with you. A strong relationship with employees yields incredible results at the workplace.

An empathetic leader creates a bond with their teammates. It's not about making them your best friend but building a bond that helps them rely on you. They can trust you with their challenges at work because you share a bond with them. This will make the working environment a safe space.

Good leaders build relationships by:

- Asking questions
- Listening carefully
- Appreciating

A strong relationship leads to maximum results and success.

Self-Assessment Questions:

1. How strong is my relationship with my team?
2. Am I aware of their goals and dreams in life?
3. Do they trust me with their challenges?
4. Are they relaxed with me?
5. Do I listen and attend to their needs?

Rate Yourself:

| 1 | 2 | 3 | 4 | 5 | 6 |

Needs improvement   Crushing it

DAY 17

EMPATHETIC LEADERS ARE HUMBLE

Leadership with empathy involves humility. Empathetic leaders are humble. Humble leaders do not only lead, they also transform. They are willing to learn from their teammates because they can't know it all. They consider the contribution of their employees because they are not proud.

"Never look down on anybody unless you're helping him up."

JESSE JACKSON

Empathetic humble leaders shift attention from themselves. They do not make every discussion about themselves. They try not to take praise for a task an employee performed. They are humans with inner strength. They know that humility is not a sign of weakness.

When leaders are humble, they are open to criticism, therefore, their employees are unafraid to communicate with them.

Humble leaders aim to serve others. They recognize, celebrate, and reward the resilience of their employees. They are approachable. If your employees are bold enough to involve you when they encounter a challenge while working, then you are not just a humble leader but an empathetic leader.

Anyone who wants to lead must be humble.

Self-Assessment Questions:

1. Am I a humble leader?
2. Do I make everything about myself?
3. How open am I to criticism??
4. Have I ever looked down on any of my employees?
5. How can I become a humble leader?

Rate Yourself:

1	2	3	4	5	6
Needs improvement					Crushing it

DAY 18

EMPATHETIC LEADERS ARE

UNDERSTANDING

An empathetic leader is understanding. There's no show of empathy without understanding. A leader who understands every one of their employees is an outstanding leader. It's not merely about understanding their personality, but also the way they feel and think.

"You can only understand people if you feel them in yourself."

JOHN STEINBECK

Empathetic leadership involves understanding an employee's needs and struggles and offering to help. It also involves understanding and appreciating their point of view even if you wouldn't put it into consideration. It not only involves understanding their needs at work, but also what they may be going through in life.

When a leader understands their employees, they

know what they are capable of and what they are not capable of. Being an understanding leader helps to know the strengths and weaknesses of your staff and how to handle them.

Understanding your employees helps you work better with them. It builds trust and relationships. It also creates a positive impact in the workspace, leading to maximum productivity and results. Employees are happy, motivated, and productive when they are understood.

Being understanding means you have every attribute of an empathetic leader, which includes self-awareness, listening, being approachable, communicating, and being kind.

Self-Assessment Questions:

1. How understanding am I as a leader?
2. Do I listen to understand, or do I listen to talk?
3. Have I ever misunderstood any of my employees?
4. Do I reason with them?
5. How can I be more understanding?

Rate Yourself:

1   2   3   4   5   6

Needs improvement   Crushing it

DAY 19

EMPATHETIC LEADERS ARE PATIENT

A successful leader is a patient leader. If you want to succeed as a leader you have to be patient, not just with your team but also with yourself. Empathetic leaders are patient with their workers. They are not in a haste to talk, rather they listen. They don't rush their team members instead they give them ample time to be more productive. They don't pressure their employees beyond their capability instead they maximize time.

"An empathic person is a good listener, patient, understanding, and kind."

LAURA RASKIN

Patient leaders know that each employee can attain results at a certain pace. So, they are patient with every one of them. Leading with patience brings respect and maximum productivity. When a leader is patient, his employees know they have been given time to work on a task, therefore, they are more productive.

Being a patient leader builds respect and reputation at work. It also brings about productivity in the workplace. A leader who is patient with himself and his employees achieves greater results. Nevertheless, they grow their team and improve their time management skills.

A leader who is patient with himself is also patient with his employees. An empathetic and patient leader:

- Builds a positive attitude in difficult situations.
- Knows how to maximize time.
- Gives room for improvement.

The best leaders are patient leaders.

Self-Assessment Questions:

1. Am I a patient leader?
2. Do I give enough time for a task?
3. What do I do when a task is not completed?
4. Do I know how to maximize time?
5. Have I ever pressured my employees beyond their capability?

Rate Yourself:

1   2   3   4   5   6

Needs improvement   Crushing it

DAY 20

EMPATHETIC LEADERS
ARE NONJUDGMENTAL

Have you ever assumed something about an employee, and it turned out to be a lie? Good leaders know when to withhold judgments. As leaders make decisions every day with every thought or conversation, it is important they put away every sentiment, think through, and rise above their insecurities.

"Before you criticize a man, walk a mile in his shoes. That way, when you do criticize him, you'll be a mile away and have his shoes."

STEVE MARTIN

Empathetic leaders are not quick to judge or criticize any of their employees. They are open-minded. When a situation arises, they listen to each of them and try to gain a profound understanding of their perspective. This way, they develop empathy towards each of their employees and judge accordingly.

Being judgmental as a leader does more bad than good. It:

- Wrecks the relationship at workplace.
- Discourages employees.
- Leads to conflict.

Leaders who judge accordingly are good decision makers. They create a working environment free from bias.

Self-Assessment Questions:

1. Do I have an open mind when making judgements?
2. Am I always quick to judge my employees?
3. Have I made any of them feel bad by judging them?
4. Do I know when to withhold judgement?
5. How can I become less judgmental?

Writing prompt:

1. Write down how you can be kind to your employees. What ways can you appreciate them? Have you ever been sensitive towards

their needs? Why?

2. How can you detect the emotions of your employees? Do you observe how they feel?

3. What is the most common reason to be dishonest with your employee? Is it worth it?

4. Do you have a strong relationship with your employees? Write down the ways you can strengthen your relationship with your employees.

5. Are you patient with your team? How can you be more patient and less judgmental?

Rate Yourself:

1	2	3	4	5	6
Needs improvement					Crushing it

DAY 21

EMPATHETIC LEADERS ARE VULNERABLE

Leadership comes with a lot of duties. And empathetic leadership? It comes with a whole lot of responsibility. Many leaders see vulnerability as weakness, but vulnerability is not weakness. A vulnerable leader is an emphatic leader.

"Outstanding leaders go out of their way to boost the self-esteem of their personnel. If people believe in themselves, it's amazing what they can accomplish."

SAM WALTON

The strength of a leader is measured by how well he can direct, motivate, and support his team. If a leader cannot direct his team, then he has no strength over them. Strength comes from vulnerability. Vulnerable leaders are honest, they take risks and embrace imperfection.

Empathetic leaders are unafraid to show their weakness. Instead, they share their ideas, experiences, shortcomings, and difficulties with their team. This way, they feel safe sharing their challenges with you knowing you will help them by providing solutions.

Can you admit whenever you make a mistake and ask for help? Being a vulnerable leader is a risk. It involves being open and honest with yourself and your team. Letting them know that nobody is perfect including you.

Vulnerability is a source of empathy, genuineness, and accountability. It builds trust and strengthens relationships between leaders and their team. When a leader is vulnerable, it shows how committed he is to success.

Self-Assessment Questions:

1. Am I afraid to be a vulnerable leader?
2. Do I admit whenever I make mistakes in front of my employees?
3. Do I share my shortcomings with them?
4. Do I share my ideas and experience with my employees?
5. Am I open-minded with them?

Rate Yourself:

1	2	3	4	5	6

Needs improvement   Crushing it

DAY 22

EMPATHETIC LEADERS ARE HONEST

A dishonest leader cannot be trusted. Empathetic leaders are honest. They are not only honest with their employees, they are also honest with themselves and their clients or consumers. Being honest builds quality relationships. No one wants to associate with a dishonest leader.

"True honesty is hard. Throughout my career, I've faced moments where I've needed to take an honest look at myself and face some very uncomfortable realities."

LES BROWN

Honest leaders lead by example. They set good examples for their teammates. They make rules and heed them. They lead the way. A leader who hasn't been caught lying is a dishonest leader.

Empathetic leaders accept their mistakes even in front of their employees. It shows how honest and trustworthy they are. When you're honest, people trust you with their challenges. They come to you for advice when they are stuck in life. Because they know you will tell them the truth.

Honest leaders carry their followers along when making decisions. They communicate their strengths, motives, challenges, and successes with their team. This shows transparency and builds connections.

Empathetic leaders have difficult and honest discussions with their team. They give honest feedback and are appreciative. They empower their employees. Being honest as a leader builds commitment and enhances teamwork. It creates a working environment with shared goals.

Self-Assessment Questions:

1. How often do I tell my employees the truth?
2. Have I ever shied away from difficult conversations?
3. Do I carry them along when making decisions?
4. Have I been dishonest with them?
5. Do I give honest feedback?

Rate Yourself:

1	2	3	4	5	6

Needs improvement   Crushing it

DAY 23

EMPATHETIC LEADERS ARE CONFIDENT

Leadership is a skill you become great at with experience. Empathetic leaders are confident. Confident leaders are good communicators, great listeners, and motivators. They are self-aware and courageous.

"A true leader has the confidence to stand alone, the courage to make tough decisions, and the compassion to listen to the needs of others. He does not set out to be a leader but becomes one by the equality of his actions and the integrity of his intent."

DOUGLAS MACARTHUR

Confident leaders are optimistic and hopeful towards the development of their organization. A self-confident leader looks confident, talks confidently, and knows what it means to be a leader. They know their strengths and weaknesses, but it doesn't define them.

How can a confident leader show empathy? Being

confident does not make you an empath, therefore, not all confident leaders are empathetic. Confident, empathetic leaders do not give up on themselves, their employees, and their organization. They believe that growth comes with time. Therefore, they give their employees time to grow.

They listen with compassion to their employees and try to relate with their specific problems. Then they motivate them to work harder in order to attain success. When success is attained, they celebrate wins. Confident leaders are focused on their growth, but empathetic leaders are concerned about the growth of their employees as well. They ensure everyone works to build a record of their wins.

Being a confident leader comes with taking risks and making good decisions for the development of your community or organization.

Self-Assessment Questions:

1. Am I a confident leader?
2. Have I given up on any of my employees?
3. How often do I give up on a goal or task?
4. Do I give my employees time to grow?
5. Am I confident enough to make tough decisions?

Rate Yourself:

| 1 | 2 | 3 | 4 | 5 | 6 |

Needs improvement   Crushing it

....

....

....

....

....

....

....

....

....

....

....

....

....

....

....

....

....

....

....

....

DAY 24

EMPATHETIC LEADERSHIP
PROMOTES EFFICIENCY

A leader who knows how to relate well with his staffers and clients produces maximum productivity for his organization. When employees know they are valued, they become more efficient. Empathetic leadership creates a positive working environment that enhances efficiency.

"There's a power in empathy."

TARANA BURKE

Studies show that employees work better when they are cared for, supported, and motivated. However, empathetic leaders identify, listen, and understand the needs of their employees. They work alongside their team, empowering them and building them for the task ahead. This promotes success and development at the workplace.

No leader wants to be a failure. Being empathetic as a leader helps to promote success. When you understand your employees and know how to solve their problems or help with their challenges at work, it increases cooperation. Cooperating as a team leads to greater achievement.

Empathetic leaders create a comfortable and peaceful environment. This helps to attain milestones, achieve shared goals, and accomplish a task effectively.

Self-Assessment Questions:

1. How have I enhanced efficiency at work?
2. Do I relate well with my staff?
3. Do I cooperate with them?
4. Have I been able to create a positive environment?
5. How can I make my employees more efficient?

Rate Yourself:

1	2	3	4	5	6

Needs improvement   Crushing it

DAY 25

EMPATHETIC LEADERS ARE FOCUSED

The best thing any leader can do for himself is to be focused. Leaders who are focused achieve anything they set their mind to. They are self-aware and emotionally intelligent. Focused leaders do not let anything distract them. They concentrate on their vision and goals. How focused are you as a leader?

"The highest form of knowledge is empathy."

BILL BULLARD

Empathetic leaders are not only focused on themselves, they are also focused on the outer world and on their employees. When a leader is focused on himself, he recognizes his inner voice and his strength. He doesn't allow the outer world to distract him. He is determined to succeed. As an emphatic leader, your focus should not only be on yourself and on the outside world, but also on the people you lead.

Studies show that leaders who have higher rank find it difficult to focus on their employees. Being focused on your employees means giving them attention and being present for them especially when they need you. You should be able to sense when they need you. If you are always there and it seems like you are not there, then it is better you are absent. Being focused on your staff builds relationships and enhances growth.

Self-Assessment Questions:

1. What can distract me from being a great leader?
2. Am I a focused leader?
3. Do I achieve anything I set my mind to?
4. How can I focus on myself and on my employees as well?
5. Do I focus on the outside world?

Rate Yourself:

1	2	3	4	5	6
Needs improvement					Crushing it

DAY 26

EMPATHETIC LEADERSHIP
LEADS TO ACCOUNTABILITY

Empathetic leadership leads to accountability. An accountable leader is a responsible leader. The first step to being accountable as a leader is to build a strong relationship with your team. Being accountable means being responsible when things go wrong even when it isn't your fault.

"When things go wrong in your command, start searching for the reason in increasingly large circles around your own desk."

GEN. BRUCE CLARKE

When a leader is accountable, he sets goals and defines the role of each team member in achieving those goals. However, he helps them by guiding them to achieve shared goals. Being accountable creates clear expectations.

Empathetic leaders strive to be accountable. They

establish a culture where employees are also held accountable when they do not complete their task. They empower their team.

They encourage their team, and this builds a high level of trust and performance. When a leader is not accountable, it leads to:

- Poor performance
- Low productivity
- Conflict
- Lack of trust
- Missed deadlines

Accountable leaders get the job done. Therefore, empathetic leaders who are accountable should create a positive working environment. This helps employees to count on one another, accomplish their duties, and feel comfortable to approach them when the need arises.

Self-Assessment Questions:

1. Am I an accountable leader?
2. Do I take responsibility when things go wrong or blame my team?

3. How well do I empower my team?
4. Who do I hold accountable when a task is not completed?
5. How can I be an accountable leader?

Rate Yourself:

1	2	3	4	5	6

Needs improvement   Crushing it

DAY 27

EMPATHETIC LEADERS ASK QUESTIONS

Curiosity is the number one attribute of an empathetic leader. The best way to communicate with your employees and understand them is to ask questions. If you cannot ask questions, how then will you find answers? You cannot detect the needs of your employees and consumers without asking them questions. Asking questions as a leader helps you know what your employees are going through. How they feel working for you and what their challenges may be.

"The purpose of human life is to serve, and to show compassion and the will to help others."

ALBERT SCHWEITZER

When you ask questions, you listen and think through on how to provide solutions to employees problems. It also helps you know what's going on with your team members: how they are accomplishing a task, what problems they may be facing in their personal life, and how you can help. Asking questions strengthens relationships at the workplace.

You never know why they haven't completed a task until you ask. You never know why they are not smiling until you ask. You never know why they are absent from work until you ask. Asking questions is an unavoidable attribute of an emphatic leader. A leader who doesn't ask questions does not care about the needs of his employees.

Self-Assessment Questions:

1. Do I care about my employees?
2. How often do I ask them how their work is going?
3. Do I assume more than I ask questions?
4. Do I know the challenges they are facing?
5. How can I ask more questions?

Rate Yourself:

1	2	3	4	5	6

Needs improvement   Crushing it

DAY 28

EMPATHETIC LEADERS ARE SUPPORTIVE

A leader who does not support his employees is not empathetic. Being supportive as a leader means you are compassionate and approachable. Supportive leaders provide resources and tools for the completion of a task. They know every employee's weaknesses and strengths and help if the need arises. They communicate and listen to their employees' needs and challenges. Then find a way to support them.

"As you grow older, you will discover that you have two hands, one for helping yourself and the other for helping others."

SAM LEVENSON

Empathetic leaders who are supportive give their time and attention to their team when they are approached to help with a challenge. They are resourceful, approachable, confident, and patient. They encourage teamwork. They ask their team to help each other when the need arises, and when they can't, they help out. They do not just give a task to their team, they see to the completion of that task.

Empathetic leaders do not only show support at work. They also help their employees to solve their personal problems.

When employees are supported, they are loyal. They feel valued and loved.

Being a supportive leader builds relationships and trust and empowers a team. It improves work performance and shows how committed a leader is to his work.

Self-Assessment Questions:

1. Do I support my employees?
2. Do I help them solve their problems or ignore them?
3. Have I ever denied them my support when they need it?
4. How can I encourage teamwork?
5. How can I be more supportive?

Rate Yourself:

1	2	3	4	5	6

Needs improvement   Crushing it

DAY 29

EMPATHETIC LEADERSHIP
SHARPENS YOUR INSIGHT

Empathetic leaders are the best leaders. Everyone wants to work with an empathetic leader. Someone who is aware of their feelings and their thoughts. A leader who supports, motivates, and appreciates them. When you listen, you learn, and when you learn, you gain insight.

"When you show deep empathy towards others, their defensive energy goes down and positive energy replaces it. That's when you can get more creative in solving problems."

STEPHEN COVEY

Being empathetic makes you a better leader. It sharpens your insights. What does this mean? Let's say an employee is absent from work without notice. A leader who is not empathetic will assume the employee is unserious and may likely yell at him or even demote him. Whereas, the first thing an empathetic leader will do is to communicate to know why that employee is absent. He asks questions, listens, and understands the reason for such misconduct.

Empathetic leaders do not judge or make assumptions. They discern, perceive, understand, and comprehend. They think before they act. They understand that nobody is perfect. They learn about their employees and understand each of them. They see inside of them and their problems.

The insightful leader sees through critical issues that may hinder progress. Being insightful helps leaders to solve problems and know how to deal with people. This helps them manage employees and clients. It also aids the success of an organization.

Self-Assessment Questions:

1. Am I an insightful leader?
2. Do I make assumptions?
3. How can I be more empathetic?
4. How can I sharpen my insight with empathy?
5. How do I gain insight?

Rate Yourself:

1	2	3	4	5	6

Needs improvement   Crushing it

DAY 30

EMPATHETIC LEADERS LEAD FROM WITHIN

Leadership comes from within. You cannot be an empathetic leader if you do not lead from within. Leaders who lead from within lead from a deep spot that lives within their hearts. They are very committed to their values and beliefs. And are focused to achieve their objectives as leaders.

"True compassion comes from free will by drawing empathy from within."

SHANE BARBI

Empathetic leaders who lead from within put their employees before themselves. They are compassionate and understanding. They are good communicators and attentive listeners. They attend to the needs of their staffers. They know what is important to them and they are focused.

Leaders who lead from within are empathetic. They examine themselves and are conscious of how they treat employees and their consumers. When leaders lead from within, they seek understanding and enhance their integrity.

Most leaders are too busy to pause and think about their inner roots and the quality of their leadership. But empathetic leaders are not. Instead, they ask themselves questions and answer them with their actions. Questions like:

- Am I a good leader?
- How can I become a better leader?
- How can I meet the expectations of those I serve?

And many more.

These questions help them become a great leader. It shows they are self-aware. It helps them know when something is wrong with their leadership. Leading from within brings clarity of vision, direction, and values. It enhances greater performance and provides strong beginnings.

Do you lead from within?

Self-Assessment Questions:

1. Do I lead from within?

2. Am I committed?
3. Am I conscious of how I treat my employees?
4. Am I too busy to pause and think of how I will become a better leader?
5. How can I lead from within?

Writing prompt:

1. Write down how you can be confident in yourself and your employees.
2. Is there a reason to be dishonest with your employee? In what ways can you be honest?
3. What distracts you from being a good leader? How can you help your team complete a task?
4. Do you support your team? What ways can you be a supportive leader?
5. What kind of leader are you? Do you have a leadership style? Write down ways you can lead from within.

Rate Yourself:

1	2	3	4	5	6
Needs improvement					Crushing it

EMPATHY QUESTIONNAIRE

Please **CHECK ONE** response that best describes you. Be honest, since the information will be used to help you become more empathetic. There are no right or wrong answers.

Student ID   **Date**

....

Not very like me → Very like me

	1	2	3	4	5
1. I try to see things from other people's points of view.	☐	☐	☐	☐	☐
2. When I don't understand someone's point of view, I ask questions to learn more.	☐	☐	☐	☐	☐
3. When I disagree with others, it's hard for me to understand their perspective.	☐	☐	☐	☐	☐
4. I consider people's circumstances when I'm talking with them.	☐	☐	☐	☐	☐

	Not very like me → Very like me				
	1	2	3	4	5
5. I try to imagine how I would feel in someone else's situation.	☐	☐	☐	☐	☐
6. When someone is upset, I try to remember a time when I felt the same way.	☐	☐	☐	☐	☐
7. When I'm reading a book or watching a movie, I think about how I would react if I was one of the characters.	☐	☐	☐	☐	☐
8. Sometimes I wonder what it would feel like to be in my parents' situation.	☐	☐	☐	☐	☐
9. When a friend is upset, I try to show them that I understand how they feel.	☐	☐	☐	☐	☐
10. I say things like "I can see why you feel that way."	☐	☐	☐	☐	☐
11. I've been known to say "You are wrong" when someone is sharing their opinion.	☐	☐	☐	☐	☐

	Not very like me → Very like me				
	1	2	3	4	5
12. When a friend or family member is sad, my actions let them know I understand (like a hug or a pat on the back).	☐	☐	☐	☐	☐
13. I say things like "Something like that happened to me once, I understand how you feel."	☐	☐	☐	☐	☐
14. I've told my friends things like, "You shouldn't be upset about that" or "Stop feeling that way."	☐	☐	☐	☐	☐
15. When I know one of my friends is upset, I try to talk to them about it.	☐	☐	☐	☐	☐

Gaumer Erickson, A.S., Soukup, J.H., Noonan, P.M., & McGurn, L. (2016). Empathy Questionnaire. Lawrence, KS: University of Kansas, Center for Research on Learning.

CREATING AN EMPATHY PICTURE

Empathy helps us understand the feelings of another person. It requires us to walk in someone else's shoes, which takes imagination (Shapiro, 2020).

The following exercise encourages us to use that imagination to build a picture of someone else's situation.

The *Creating an Empathy Picture* worksheet includes five steps and can be made appropriate to any age group and used in individual or group sessions.

Ask the person or group to:

1. Cut out a picture from a newspaper or magazine with an individual in a scene (for example, a person at a bus stop, leaving a shop, or boarding a plane).

2. Stick the picture on a larger sheet of paper.

3. Ask questions about the person and their life and imagine possible answers:

- Who is this person? Give them a name, a family (or none), a job, and even finances.
- What decision do they need to make, or what do they need to do?
- What is impacting their decision (either within or outside the picture)?
- What might they say?
- What are others telling them to do (friends, colleagues, partner)?
- What do we imagine they will do?

4. Write down the answers in the space left around the picture.

5. The situation can be entirely the product of the person's imagination as they look at the picture or drawn from their circumstances.

References:

Shapiro, S. L. (2020). Rewire your mind: Discover the science + practice of mindfulness. London: Aster.

EMPATHY BINGO

Empathy Bingo can be played in group therapy contexts, or by an individual on their own. Designed to help players differentiate between empathy and other responses, this handout has two parts:

- **Part A** is a bingo grid that lists different types of responses that are common during interactions. Cross out each square as you recognize a certain type of response from Part B. If you are working in a group setting, you may want to copy the sheet so that each group member has their own bingo grid.

- **Part B** is a set of snippets from different example dialogues – therapists can read these out to a group, or individuals can cover the left-hand column and read through them without seeing the answers. Each snippet corresponds to a different square on the grid – that is, a dialogue may exemplify "Correcting," "Educating," and so forth.

This exercise can help you or a group learn about the different ways we can respond to a friend in need of empathy, and why empathy is usually the best choice.

Part A

Interrogating	One-Upping	Advising	Correcting
Consoling	Shutting Down	Educating	Sympathizing
Explaining	Fixing It	Empathizing	Storytelling

Part B

Fixing It	A: I'm anxious about getting to the airport on time. B: I'll drive you.
One-Upping	A: Check out this bruise from my fall down the stairs. B: That's tiny, look at what I got when I was hit by a bike.
Storytelling	A: I couldn't get a taxi for hours last night and had to walk home at 5 am. B: That sounds like the time when...

Consoling	A: I feel terrible that my student failed his exam. B: You're not to blame, you're a brilliant tutor.
Sympathizing	A: The dentist told me I need to have very painful root canal surgery. B: Oh man, that's terrible.
Interrogating	A: I can't get my mom to listen to my point of view. B: What's the problem, exactly?
Shutting Down	A: My boss has cut my pay. B: Buck up, let's play some pool.
Educating	A: I don't know anybody at my new college. B: See it as a chance to develop your social skills.
Explaining	A: I'm annoyed because you left the kids waiting an hour after school. B: That's only because the traffic was terrible...
Advising	A: I can't understand where all my money goes after I get paid. B: I reckon you should create a budget.
Correcting	A: I think your essay about the greenhouse could be improved. B: It was about a glasshouse, not a greenhouse.
Empathizing	A: My whole house is flooded and everything in it is soaked. B: Do you feel stressed out and in need of some support?

TELLING AN EMPATHY STORY

Empathy is an integral part of social and emotional development and an essential motivator for helping those in distress. In a very literal sense, it is the *"ability to feel or imagine another person's emotional experience"* (McDonald & Messinger, 2011).

Telling someone else's story can be an excellent way to understand other perspectives while developing empathy.

The Telling a Story worksheet includes five steps that can be used in individual or group sessions:

1. Identify a story. It could be a family member, a newspaper clip, or a biography.
2. Choose a medium. How do you want to tell the story?
    A. Art (cartoons, drawings, collages, etc.)
    B. Newspaper article, poetry, or dramatic story
    C. Video, narration, and music
3. Use your own words and style to try and focus on

how the person feels, what emotions they were going through, what fears and hopes they have.

4. Share the story with someone and explain what you think they feel and why.

5. Ask the other person what they think of the story and what emotions they saw in it.

References:

McDonald, N. M., & Messinger, D. S. (2011). The Development of Empathy: How, When, and Why. Retrieved September 01, 2020, from https://www.researchgate.net/publication/267426505_The_Development_of_Empathy_How_When_and_Why

LISTENING ACCURATELY WORKSHEET

#1: Step In Their Shoes

Select someone that you would like to work on your relationship with.

When you talk, try your best to take their point of view. For instance, try picturing that you are them, going about their day. Does your capacity to feel empathy change by taking their perspective?

#2: Fact-Check Your Interpretations

Reflect on the dialogues you and that person have had. Make a conscious effort to fact-check your interpretations and assumptions regarding what they said.

#3: Give Your Full Attention

During a conversation, start by giving your full attention to the other person. Before you move on to other things, consider what might occur if you asked: "I would like to clarify that I've understood you correctly. May I?" Almost every time, you'll get a positive response.

#4: Clarify What They've Said

Make an effort to clarify what you think you have heard – identify and reflect their emotions. If you are unsure whether you've understood correctly, just ask.

#5: Clarify What You've Said

During conversations, you might try asking the speaker if they could share what they've heard from you. How would you clear up any misunderstandings if they arose?

FIRST IMPRESSIONS

Purpose

To get participants moving around and introduced to each other.

Materials Required

1. Name card for each person.
2. Markers.
3. Paper and pencils/pens.

Preparation

Have participants fill out their name card.

Activity

Ask participants to form pairs. Explain that you are going to ask participants to guess their partners' favorite things. As you call out items, participants will write their guesses on paper.

For example, you might say: What would you guess is your partner's favorite?

- TV show
- Vacation destination
- Food
- Sport
- Hobby

Give participants a few seconds or so to write each response. When you have gone through your list, ask participants to share their guesses with their partners.

After participants have had a couple of minutes to share their guesses, you might ask:

1. What did you base your guesses on?
2. Did anyone guess everything wrong? Did anyone guess everything right?

Wrap up by making the point that in any personal interaction, first impressions are often misleading. When we start a negotiation, the guesses we make about another person can lead to false assumptions about what the person wants.

WORKSHEET: EXPRESS YOURSELF

Read through the following scenarios. Write your first response to each. Do not overanalyze the scenario or answer it with what sounds the best. Give your honest feedback.

1. You are the team lead for a project at work and your boss yells at you because it was not completed by the required deadline. You:

....

....

....

....

....

....

....

....

....

....

2. You find out that several of your co-workers are talking about you behind your back to the boss. They are telling your boss that you are slacking on the job and that the quality of your work is poor. You:

....

....

....

....

....

3. One of the company's clients called and told your manager that you were very rude to him. You know the client spoke to a co-worker who sits next to you, not you. You:

....

....

....

....

....

WORKSHEET: EMPATHY IS KEY

Read through the following statements and circle the most empathetic response.

1. I can't believe Mr. Smith is making me work third shift. He knows I have children.

   A. Mr. Smith is running a business and we have to do what we have to do.

   B. I can understand why you would be upset. Have you tried asking him if he could switch you to an earlier shift?

   C. I would be happy if I got third shift since there is a pay differential.

2. I have too much work on my plate.

   A. I'm sorry you feel overwhelmed by the amount of work you have. Is there any way I can help?

   B. That's good since so many people are unemployed right now.

   C. Complete the projects you can and discard the rest.

3. I am so upset. I thought I was going to get the job promotion.

    A. The better candidate got the job.
    B. Start spreading rumors about the work performance of the one who got it, and then maybe they will give it to you.
    C. I know you are disappointed about not getting the job, but don't give up. There will be a posting of a similar position next week, apply for it.

4. The regional meeting ran over time, now I will be late for my team meeting.

    A. At least we had time to discuss all of our quarterly goals in the regional meeting.
    B. I apologize for you being tardy. Is it possible for John to share with you his notes from the first ten minutes of the meeting?
    C. The regional manager is only in town once a quarter, we needed to accommodate her.

5. I am unable to meet my quota this month.

    A. Maybe we should promote Sarah to your position.

B. Is that because you were wasting time?

C. Let's talk about why you were unable to meet your quota. What can we do to ensure this does not happen next month?

WORKSHEET: SELF-MANAGEMENT SKILLS

The following personal skills are important to effective self-management. Read through each skill and write a one to two sentence definition. Once you have defined each skill, create a scenario in which the use of the skill would be important.

1. Reflection

....

....

....

....

2. Self-Awareness

....

....

....

....

3. Planning

....

....

....

....

4. Monitoring

....

....

....

....

5. Time Management

....

....

....

....

6. Flexibility

....

....

....

....

7. Self-Appraisal

....

....

....

....

WORKSHEET:
HOW AWARE ARE YOU?

Read through the list of personal characteristics. Circle the ten that most describe you. Of those ten, put a star beside the top five characteristics you exhibit the majority of the time.

- Academic
- Active
- Accurate
- Adventurous
- Aggressive
- Ambitious
- Bold
- Broad-minded
- Calm
- Clear-thinking
- Competitive
- Confident
- Cooperative
- Determined
- Dependable
- Efficient

- Enthusiastic
- Firm
- Flexible
- Honest
- Independent
- Logical
- Meticulous
- Organized
- Practical
- Quick
- Rational
- Resourceful
- Responsible
- Sensible
- Stable
- Tactful

- Teachable
- Trustworthy
- Understanding

WORKSHEET: AGREE TO DISAGREE

Read through the following scenarios. Each partner must take a side and then engage in a dialogue where both sides constructively disagree.

1. Your boss feels that you should be demoted to a lesser position because you don't seem to be comfortable with a position of authority. You disagree and have several examples of times when you had to use your authority to make sure tasks were completed.

2. You created a training manual for your department and wrote a section that talks about the pros and cons of working in a particular position, mentioned by employees who are currently in the role. The training manager says that this is inappropriate and must be removed.
   You disagree and explain why you feel this information is beneficial to all involved.

3. The policy changed and instead of taking a

written message from a client who is calling for an employee who is not at his / her desk, you must forward clients' calls to the employee's voicemail so they can leave a voice message.

You disagree that this is the best way to handle the situation because it's possible for the machine not to record the message.

4. Your supervisor has requested that everyone come in on Saturday and work 8 hours in order to finish a project. You disagree that this is the most sensible use of time and suggest that everyone work 1 hour to 1.5 hours additionally each day of the week until the project is complete.

WORKSHEET:
SAY WHAT YOU MEAN

Read through the scenarios and verbally respond using the specified emotion.

1. You were recently offered a position within the company that pays more but also requires greater responsibility, responsibilities that you don't believe you can handle.

   Respond in a happy manner: I am so grateful for this opportunity and look forward to joining the team.

   Respond in an apprehensive manner: I am so grateful for this opportunity and look forward to joining the team.

   Respond in a confused manner: I am so grateful for this opportunity and look forward to joining the team.

2. You just found out one of your weakest team members is leaving the company. You tell him:

   Respond in an angry manner: I am so sad to see you go.

   Respond in an indifferent manner: I am so sad to see you go.

   Respond in a worried manner: I am so sad to see you go.

3. You have been put on a verbal warning due to your tardiness. You say:

   Respond in a sincere manner: I truly apologize for my tardiness. It will not happen again.

   Respond in a defensive manner: I truly apologize for my tardiness. It will not happen again.

   Respond in a carefree manner: I truly apologize for my tardiness. It will not happen again.

WORKSHEET:
IS THE GLASS HALF FULL?

Read through the following statements and verbally give a positive response to each statement.

1. The morale of the team is down.

2. We have to work overtime this weekend.

3. My quality level is 1 percentage point below the requirement.

4. The training class does not understand the material they are being taught.

5. This work environment is too fast-paced.

6. This department may be downsizing.

7. Several people got upset in today's meeting.

8. My computer is moving slowly.

9. We did not receive all of the reference material we need to complete the project.

10. The manager's instructions are not clear.

RECOMMENDED READING LIST

Blake, C. (2009) The Art of Decisions: How to Manage in an Uncertain World.

Bradberry, T. and Greaves, J. (2007) The Emotional Intelligence Quick Book: Everything You Need to Know to Put Your EQ to Work [Audiobook] [CD] (Audio CD).

Carnegie, D. (2009) How to Win Friends and Influence People.

Covey, S. (2004) The 7 Habits of Highly Effective People.

Csikszentmihalyi, M. (2008) Flow: The Psychology of Optimal Experience.

Deci, E. and Flaste, R. (1996) Why We Do What We Do: Understanding Self-Motivation.

Dweck, C. (2000) Self-theories: Their Role in Motivation, Personality, and Development (Essays in Social Psychology).

Goleman, D. (2000) Working with Emotional Intelligence.

Klemmer, B. (2007) The Compassionate Samurai: Being Extraordinary in an Ordinary World.

Nuernberger, P. (2003) Strong and Fearless.

Segal, Jeanne S. (1997) Raising Your Emotional Intelligence: A Practical Guide.

Seligman, M. (1998) Learned Optimism: How to Change Your Mind and Your Life.

What people are saying about empathetic leadership

Empathetic leaders understand and value the way that others see the world. Empathetic leaders love all people.

IAN EISHEN

Empathic leaders try to truly put themselves in the individual's situation(s). As well as assist that person in navigating said situation with compassion, support and understanding.

LAGINA BELTRAN

When someone cuts me off here in San Antonio. Instead of getting mad, I just tell myself that maybe they have to go to the restroom really bad. I've been there, I empathize with them.

MATT HERNANDEZ

They stay in the present and remain free of judgement.

ARTIE PEARSON

Empathetic leaders value differences.

EDWIN LUDWIGSEN

Empathetic leaders meet people where they're at. They go all the way to meet people at their points of need. Empathetic leaders just don't call across the scary rope bridge and tell you it's going to be okay, they cross the bridge first to help you across.

JEREMY LINDNER

Empathetic leaders celebrate inclusion and guide with compassion.

ASHLEY HARGROVE

Bring truthful but optimistic energy by being positive.

RODNEY B. FLOYD

Empathetic leaders understand the needs of others to help them become successful.

SOPHIE HUNT

Not judging what I am walking through.

DERICA MCCAGHREN

Empathetic leaders connect with people and care for them in the times they need them.

DANIEL VILLEGAS

Empathetic leaders work alongside their team. Not ahead, not behind, but with. They understand what their team is going through in order to effectively lead them.

RHONDA RUSSELL

Empathetic leaders are nonjudgmental - Empathetic leaders don't rush towards judgement. They meet you head on with an open mind and an open heart. See me, hear me, understand me, then meet me where I am.

VERONICA HASKIN

Empathetic leaders take into account that everyone has a story. They not only want to hear that story, but truly understand it as well.

JASON DELUCY

Empathetic leaders...
- Understand that they don't have all the answers
- Empower and build
- Don't always lead from the front
- Understand the importance of followership
- Are works in progress

ABI SCOTT

Empathetic leaders demand accountability.

MIKE DUGAN

Empathetic leaders take the time to hear the person that's going through their life challenges and help them bounce back up from a "bottom" that they don't see past.

Empathetic leaders give the person a safe place to have a sounding board free of judgement but with free honesty.

Empathetic leaders are also someone that can be an example of what to do or not do when going through whatever the situation is.

CANDI SCHNEIDER

Empathetic leaders are approachable and non judgmental.

IVAN ACOSTA

Empathetic leaders are present and relatable... inclusive... genuinely care...create a space where people feel safe and can open up. Don't rush to make others understand, because they are first understanding.

KEYONA CAMPBELL

- Listens.
- Focused on support vs fixing the problem.
- Able to learn from everyone.

SHERONNE KING

Empathetic leaders will often put others' needs ahead of their own for the greater good of the organization.

TYLER DUNCAN

Many layers to this.

It is not all encompassing within one person. It's not the personality of everyone, and that's ok. Empathetic leaders genuinely value the lens of others and have the ability to reach—teach and release the team around them with feeling.

DANNY DAVIS

Empathetic leaders lead with unbiased intentions. They're well aware of what's above the left breast pocket, but they're fueled by what's about the right.

MICHAEL DENSON

Empathetic leaders empathize with themselves, first.

RYAN NATALINI

Empathetic leaders learn about and know their team members.

WENDY MCCOLLUM

Being an empathetic leader doesn't mean you know what someone has experienced but that you can relate emotionally to the excitement, sadness, anger, overwhelming sense of their being and that you are their person. Their person that listens, that believes, that cannot imagine but can see. You are the person that just happens to be aware and not in the know but present in the moment.

CAROLYN PHILLIPS

Empathic leaders are aware of the needs of others, listen and consider what others say, and are able to understand both the verbal and non-verbal reactions of others.

MICHELE BRYANT

Empathetic leaders understand that not everything needs an answer.

DAVANN IRONS

Empathetic leaders genuinely care.

VERONICA TANNERY

Empathetic leaders lead from the front, love from the center, and celebrate from the back.

ADAM JOACHIM

Empathetic leaders are active listeners when

their people need them. They don't need to provide recommendation or advice but simply lend an ear to their members.

JIMMY TRAN

Empathetic leaders default to rehabilitation.

SHANE P LM

Empathetic leaders don't just meet people where they are, they accompany them on the journey.

DEMETRIUS BOOTH

Empathetic leaders understand the challenges others face and thus create for them an environment to thrive.

GEORGE "STEVE" CUM

Ability to understand the needs of others without judgement.

MANNY PIÑEIRO

Empathetic leaders have a power in their example that reaches far beyond the authority of their rank.

BOBBY KAZMIR

Empathetic leaders know their teams and set them up for success with their natural skill sets as well as strengthening their weaknesses. They also can recognize when they or a teammate needs to take a knee.

MICHAEL WALSH

Empathic leaders are honest.

LOWELL BIGFISH

To be an empathetic leader, you have to do the following...
Stop - Drop everything and focus on subordinate.
Listen - Do not be pre-occupied during

the engagement. Devote total attention to

the engagement. Devote total attention to subordinate.

Seek to Understand - Try to define the issue at hand.

Be Nonjudgmental - Leave biases behind and approach with an open mind.

Exercise Emotional Intelligence - Leave emotions behind and don't let your preferences become your prejudices.

Reflection - Look at your past and seek similar experiences in an effort to better understand.

Assist - Help subordinate get to a state of success.

Follow-up - Circle back to subordinate to ensure a successful/satisfactory state has been achieved.

DARYL CORNETT

Empathetic leaders know feelings aren't weakness and allow them to aid inquiry within their leadership teams.

KIMBERLY POLLARD

Empathetic leaders value and recognize the importance of other people's emotions.

RAUL J. TORRES

Empathetic leaders are who they once needed.

DEONDRA PARKS

Empathetic leaders are the G.O.A.T! They are relatable because they've "been there and done that" and understand their journey can help guide those that follow them. They've mastered the ability to hold you accountable in a way YOU are able to receive and develop from. They are compassionate and are a necessity in any organization.

SHA-NIA PORTER

Empathetic leaders are open-minded and non judgmental. They welcome conversations no matter how difficult they may be.

KHAMILLIA WASHINGTON

Empathetic leaders build you up not by holding your hand, but by giving you a safe environment to grow.

STEVE KRISTY ISHMAEL

Empathetic leaders are compassionate and have strong emotional intelligence.

DON BROWN

Empathic leaders go where the hurt is, not only at work but where families are in pain like the ER. Empathic leaders value airmen and their families to get this mission accomplished!

LEN ARSENAULT

Empathetic leaders must be Humble, Credible and Visible.

KEVIN LOMBARDO

Empathetic leaders support you in your time of need.

PAULA V. TUDOR

Empathetic leaders are vulnerable, trustworthy humans who see and feel through the lens of other but truly understand it as well.

TRICIA MARIE

Empathetic leaders: THINK-ACT- DO.

KEITH CASTILLE

Empathetic leaders are not always the subject matter experts, rather they understand talent and where to move people within their team. They maximize their people's potential while ensuring the mission and unit needs are being met. They collaborate, they connect, and they move through their days unapologetically by that which sets their souls on fire.

JANEE WALKER

Empathetic leaders feel without the need to be felt.

EBONI REAMS

Empathetic leaders do not feel the need to scramble to find a similar story to relate to others. They know that it's more important to walk beside you in your journey than it is to have walked in your shoes.

GLORIA LINETTE WEATHERSPOON

Empathetic leaders connect with a path that is direct. No BS, no games. Unfiltered heart to heart interaction.

KEITH CASTILLE

Empathetic leaders are present in the moment to listen, care and value the walk the other person is going through.

CRIS TINA

Empathetic leaders strive to get the best out of their team because they are not blind to the internal and external struggles that disrupt our personnel.

NATHANIEL RONEY

Empathetic leaders create emotional and psychological safety.

DELILAH ALVARADO

Empathetic leaders make time for people over processes.

MONICA LUNA

Empathetic leaders share in another's emotions through a foundation of trust and honesty.

JEFFREY BANKOSKE

Empathetic leaders have a heartfelt consideration for others' well-being.

RODNEY BRYANT

Empathetic leaders meet people where they are, and are willing to just be with them, and listen without judging them.

JENNY PATTERSON

Empathetic leaders may not always understand what another is feeling but aren't afraid to make themselves vulnerable in order to do so.

KIAH KENT

Empathetic leaders own their mindset. Empathetic leaders meet their people where they are in their honest truth and that begins with having an open, unbiased, unclouded mindset to accept another's testimony. Only then can a leader begin to truly empathize, and it all begins with the mindset.

TERESA WEST

Empathetic leaders are guided by their instinct of tried-and-true leadership understanding (True North). People want to follow them for their moral worth not their authority.

MICHAEL WAYNE

Empathetic leaders KNOW it's never about them. They not only take the time to invest in you, but also your family.

LATONIA BOOZE

Empathetic leaders meet their people where they are at.

JENNIFER KERSEY

Empathic leaders use the pain, grief, loss, trauma, and failure they've experienced to transparently and authentically connect with where their people are hurting.

AARON MOLCHAK

Empathetic leaders are approachable.
Empathetic leaders possess cultural competence.
Empathetic leaders are active listeners.

Empathetic leaders tend to possess the characteristics of being global citizens.

BEVERLY DAVISON-HILL

Seeing another and the turmoil they are going through even though it may or may not be of their own making.

TOR BLACK

Empathic leaders leave their ego at the door.

RITCHIE BROWN

Empathetic leaders cultivate inclusivity by understanding opposing views (understanding doesn't require complete acceptance).

KENDALL BRISCOE

Empathetic leaders are present.

BRIAN SHEFFIELD

Empathetic leaders put themselves in others' shoes to understand better.

ALLAN MACK

Empathy is not being a psychopath.

CALEB SUTTON

Empathetic leaders understand that everyone has flaws. They build on those flaws to create progress!

CHRIS SIROTKIN

Empathetic leaders have the heart of a lion and ears of a mouse. The courage to journey to unfamiliar territory and attention to hear the equivocal cry for help.

RYAN TAYLOR

Empathetic leaders take the time necessary to know and understand themselves through periods of personal reflection. They know that self-awareness of their personal biases, strengths, and weaknesses permits them the courage to be more vulnerable with their teammates, which improves their ability to connect with others. They stay attune to their environment and deliberately seek feedback to improve how they interact with those they serve with an open-minded approach.

ADAM BOUBEDE

Removing yourself and your personal feeling or bias from the situation. To be an empathetic leader is to try and understand what the other person is going through. Not to make them believe you know or that you've been exactly where they are. We, too, often, try and relate when in reality everyone's situation is unique. Pain, joy, sorrow, success are all felt different by different people. As leaders our goal should be to guide by example and yes, lend our experiences and stories to those we support and serve, but we must not be so presumptuous that we think we know exactly what they are feeling. Don't think immediately of how you will relate but listen first and then make the connection.

DAVID NAJERA

Empathetic leaders care because they don't forget where they came from. Show up for yourself and troops! People 1st-msn always.

NICK FASOLA

Empathetic leaders follow up to reassure your problem or solution is not just a check box.

STEVE DALE

Empathetic leaders are willing to understand beyond their own point of view. Their willingness to step out and meet you halfway is key to bridging "how you feel" and "how can I help."

BLACQ JAK

The ability to set aside your own understanding of life and experience it through the eyes of another.

WILLIAM HORAY

Empathetic leaders guide, uplift and encourage their people.

STEVE ARBONA

Empathetic leaders view their team members' challenges through the lens of compassion.

PAT SHAW

Empathetic leaders have recognition of all things involved and understand being most empathetic of the goal.

S. TRAVIS LEE

An empathetic leader must be a servant leader.

KENN CLIFF

Emphatic leaders show concern and emotions listen with patience, and are free of judgement.

LYNN ALLEN

Empathetic leaders are self-assured and not threatened by others' emotions, but rather seek to understand them.

MARY POLANCO

Empathetic leaders have the highest level of integrity and are respected by both his/her peers and subordinates. At the same time he/she shares the respect to all.

SAMUEL L. CANNON

Intuitive, competent, and accountable.

DREW JAMES

Empathic leaders understand the value of people is important and they take action to show members they are an asset to the team. Empathetic leaders recognize the need for diversity and inclusiveness of representation.

LINDSAY GUTIERREZ

Empathy is suspending your worldview and understanding another's, through theirs.

MATTHEW FILSINGER

Empathetic leaders are aware of their own shortcomings.

CHARMAINE REARDON KELLEY

Emphatic leaders understand and lead others to what they need. They know that an individual will always go for what they want and emphatic leaders push them to what they need.

LIMUEL GARCIA BELTRAN

...are self-aware of their own shortfalls while they lead, mentor and sometimes discipline.

JIM DAMATO

Empathic leaders fight to remain focused on others especially when their own or another experience/situation is relevant.

TONY AUGUSTINE

Empathetic leaders listen to their people and do not sympathize, it helps to understand by empathizing. We do not experience what others may do we empathize to understand and show how we care by actively listening. Also you leave your perspective out and no judgement. Being neutral helps being empathetic.

RON DUNN

Empathetic leaders don't make snap judgments.

ERIC PAXTON

Empathetic leaders drive sustained organizational success and are the glue that holds strong teams together. In other words they understand their workforce more so ideally they create the balance needed to project strong, long-term, measurable, organizational results.

SHANE OK

Empathetic leaders are intentional and deliberate with their approach; for they know far too well the feeling of being underappreciated.

DAUNTE-ANIECE SALOY

Empathetic leaders are REAL....you can spot them from miles away. They are the ones who don't need the buy-in from other folks and will keep it real with you while having a full understanding of what it feels like to be in your shoes......PERIOD

MIA AISHA

Empathetic leaders know the difference between "I had to learn the lesson when I came up" versus "You won't have to because I learned the lesson when I came up."

ADAM SHURA

Empathetic leaders meet people where they are in their life and journey. These leaders make people feel seen and heard. Lastly, empathetic leaders have the ability to be tough and hold people accountable while rebuilding one's confidence.

DON CLAYBORN

Empathetic leaders are willing to suffer with you empathetic leaders take the time to get to know their people. Empathetic leaders understand that frustration and anger is part of the process.

MICHAEL MCPHERSON

Empathetic leaders are servant leaders who lead with compassion and not an iron fist. They want to do right more than be right! They search for ways to help build life skills, not just leading skills.

ANGELA SEGAR TURHAN

The empathetic leader seeks to understand their followers beyond what many think is necessary, because the empathic leader understands that if they can locate your why the rest is easy!

HAMZA KHABIR

Empathetic leaders are willing to go the extra mile, by listening to the unspoken answer and asking the probing questions.

ROSA LAWTON

Approachable and Available...like a 7/11 that's open 24/7!

JONATHON PARKER

I think a key part that is overlooked when it comes to empathy is acknowledging another person's individual struggle. Too many times I've witnessed people dismiss someone's struggle because they feel that they've been through more difficult things in their own life and somehow that invalidates and makes another person's struggle less significant. There is nothing more frustrating than feeling as if you haven't been heard, and the quickest way to do that is to show a lack of empathy.

EVA KATHRINE HENRY

Empathetic leaders are human.

ADANDA FONDON

Empathetic leaders have a keen eye to see things from a different lens while ensuring unconditional compassion for others.

ANTHONY DUPLECHAIN

Empathetic leaders are humble. With appropriate humility, you learn from anyone. Empathetic leaders must get outside of themselves and see things from someone

else's perspective. "It's not about self."

DRE THOMAS

Empathetic leaders make time for others and themselves.

JESSICA MOHNEY MCWAIN

Empathetic leaders must have a strong sense of self-awareness. They must know how to suspend judgement, listen openly, and make no assumptions.

CHRIS MOORE

THANK YOU

Thank you to the thousands around the world that continue to support our mission to build a global network of courageous and resilient leaders.

Thank you to my amazing team and partners at Courageous Leadership Alliance. This has been an amazing journey and we are only getting started.